Praise for Midlife Magic

"By sharing her personal ups and downs, Laura Lee Carter gives us a decidedly upbeat look at how to survive and thrive while we navigate the challenges of midlife. Wonderful insights, frank observances and straight talk are the hallmark of her book. This is a collection of real-life moments that any women going through midlife can relate to."

—Maggie Rose Crane, author of *Amazing Grays: A Woman's Guide to Making the Next 50 the Best 50*

"Like a scrapbook of snapshots, Midlife Magic recounts a long journey through a series of adventures in self-discovery. It will certainly help a guy understand what all the fuss is about."

—Philip B. Persinger, author of *Do the Math: A Novel of the Inevitable*

"Midlife Magic reads like a talk with a good friend who really, really gets it. Instead of judgment and criticism for all the crazy thoughts and feelings that come with the territory of midlife, we get support, understanding and a conspiratorial, 'I know exactly how you feel!' . . . Using advice, thought-provoking ideas and humble story telling, Midlife Magic inspires and guides us as we do the work of our own midlife transition."

—Karen Hamilton, author of the blog *The Best Kept Secret*

"Midlife Magic is a frank (and often funny) examination of the challenges faced by millions of "middle-aged" adults, including those of the author, the self-proclaimed "Midlife Crisis Queen!" This book helps to clear away some of the questions over when midlife begins and adds clarity to the term "midlife crisis," revealing the phenomenon to be a new chance for self-discovery and an opportunity for us to take conscious responsibility for the rest of our lives."

—Brenda Friedrich, author of the blog *Enroute 365*

"*Laura Lee Carter generously opens up her life and tells a tale of how she faced a confluence of life-altering events—a layoff after 25 years, a divorce, a hysterectomy—to rise like a phoenix from these midlife ashes. This book is inspiring and engaging. I almost feel as if I want to experience these same kinds of dramatic circumstances so that I can start all over again, based on her example and advice.*"

—Rhea Becker, author of the blog *The Boomer Chronicles*

"*Laura Lee makes her own midlife lessons—although difficult— seem essential, achievable, even appealing. I laughed my way through the pages, learning every step of the way. This book is a delight!*"

—Katy Piotrowski, career counselor and author

The Midlife Crisis Queen's

Midlife Magic

Becoming the Person

You Are Inside!

Laura Lee Carter

MIMBRES PUBLISHING • Silver City, NM

The Midlife Crisis Queen's Midlife Magic:
Becoming the Person You Are Inside

Copyright © 2008 by Laura Lee Carter

Mimbres Publishing
PO Box 1244
Silver City, NM 88062

ISBN: 0-9658404-2-5

To my parents, Jack and Martha,
who taught me the power of the word;
and my husband, Mike,
who inspired me to use it.

Contents

"There came a time when the risk to remain tight in the bud was more painful than the risk it took to blossom." —*Anais Nin*

Introduction

Why should you care about midlife crisis? Perhaps because it can be one of the most crucial transitions of your entire life and finally lead you to true fulfillment. Is the best yet to come? You decide!

When I think back to where I was in the year 2000, in the midst of the worst of my midlife changes, I'm totally amazed at how it all turned out. There were many times I felt lost, hopeless, and alone in this journey, but I didn't give up. Eyes on the prize, even when it seems like an impossible dream!

A midlife crisis is a wake-up call to change the things in our lives that haven't been working for years but have just seemed too hard to do anything about. Things like difficult emotions, spouses, and careers. It is a timely, natural awakening that tells us we only have so many years left, so if we're going to change, the moment is now. It also invites us to be adventurous and attempt a "do-over" before it's all over.

The idea of midlife crisis has been deeply rooted in American culture since it was first mentioned in scholarly research in the 1960s and then in 1976 in Gail Sheehy's best seller *Passages: Predictable Crises of Adult Life*. But back then, the crises were all for men and were seen as silly self-indulgences (red sports cars!) driven by a fear of aging and impending death. Women were thought to develop differently and were therefore relegated to mere supporting roles, as either the victims of men's midlife crises or as "trophy wives."

Thankfully, we *have* come a long way, baby! Women stopped listening to the "experts" years ago and instead began acknowledging their own spontaneous midlife epiphanies. These life transitions have catapulted them into whole new ways of looking at meaning and purpose in midlife.

Sue Shellenbarger, in her groundbreaking 2005 study, *The Breaking Point: How Today's Women Are Navigating Midlife Crisis,* found that a startlingly high number of Americans have experienced what they consider to be a midlife crisis, broadly defined as a "stressful or turbulent psychological transition that occurs most often in the late forties or early fifties."

The data showed that by age fifty, more women than men report experiencing a turbulent midlife transition—a full 36 percent, compared with 34 percent of men. Applying these findings to the 42 million women who are nearing or in midlife today, it can be assumed that more than 15 million women will have or are presently experiencing what they consider to be a midlife crisis.

Most disturbing is the apparent cultural bias against accepting that women think and feel deeply enough to question their choices in midlife and make the needed changes at that time.

Triggers That Set Us Up for a Midlife Crisis

Any number of life crises may occur to make us suddenly and completely realize how unhappy we are with where we are in our lives. The more common ones are divorce, or the need to consider divorce; job loss; the death of a parent; career change; empty nest; and sudden, unexpected injury or illness or a near death experience.

Any change or combination of changes that are difficult to deal with and therefore wake us up with the realization that this is not the life we had pictured for ourselves—these are the events that set us on a path toward crisis and eventual life transformation.

Women's triggers are most likely a family event or problem, from a divorce or a parent's death to an extramarital affair. Male midlife crisis is more likely to be driven by work or career concerns; Women's turmoil is more likely to be driven by introspection, and women are more likely to attribute their crisis to some new insight about themselves through religion, therapy or reflection. A realization of failure in meeting parenting goals, for example, is more likely to surface in a woman. Women are also more likely than men to cite personal health problems as the cause of their crisis, including worries about physical attractiveness.

Not surprisingly, those with higher-level life skills—as in communication, relationships, and work—have a much better chance of making the life changes that will enable them to emerge from midlife more satisfied and successful.

The Queen Is Crowned
Soon after I began writing professionally, I decided to crown myself *The Midlife Crisis Queen* and launched my blog, www. MidlifeCrisisQueen.com. Why? Because I felt I had recently

experienced just about every change possible in my life. I knew it was high time for me to step up and offer support and encouragement to anyone else who might feel like a midlife loser. Little did I know what a positive, community-building experience a blog could be!

I wanted to bolster those whose courage was faltering and tell them not to give up on their craziest aspirations and ideals just because they were going through a bad patch. A recent blog comment explains perfectly why I love my work. A reader wrote, *"You have touched my life like no one has. Thank you for your insight!"*

I believe we all have boundless potential to change—at any age—and to discover a life we can only imagine now. Midlife is a great time to start manifesting the unique vision we've been secretly nurturing for years.

In this book I reveal my own personal journey through midlife change, interwoven with powerful psychological insights. My goal is to teach you how to navigate new waters with increased self-assurance, confidence, and self-respect, and come out the other end of your own midlife crisis loving yourself like never before!

The time is now! There is no past, no future, there is only this moment. So spend some time reading this book and trying to figure out what you *really* want to happen in your life right now. Start imagining your best life today. What would it take to follow through in some small way on your best life scheme and change everything? All you have to lose is your unhappiness!

I'm learning more every day through my midlife transition. It's been such an important time of self-discovery in my own life. I hope you find the same in yours!

Good luck & happy transitioning,
Laura Lee Carter, freelance writer & researcher
www.lauraleecarter.com

As life goes on it becomes tiring to keep up the character you invented for yourself, and so you relapse into individuality and become more like yourself every day. This is sometimes disconcerting for those around you, but a great relief to the person concerned. —Agatha Christie

My Story: Taking the Leap to Save My Soul

Did you ever jump off a cliff with the crazy plan to build your wings on the way down? Then you know exactly what divorce feels like.

On February 14th, 2001, the movers came, carried my life out into the street, loaded it onto their truck, and drove away. Thus began my transition from a moribund marriage to the single life again. On that day I moved into a dark, run-down, 1960s ranch-style house. It may have been Valentine's Day, but this was no sweetheart deal.

"I think I'll take my foolish heart, my friend, and head right for the door" goes the bluegrass song, and by the time I was driving down the foothills into town with my Subaru stuffed to the roof, I couldn't keep from belting out those words myself. I was scared to death, but in a good way. I was finally doing what I needed to, taking care of my precious self.

It's not like I hadn't lived alone most of my adult life, but the divorce was traumatic all the same. I couldn't kick that troublesome feeling of failure.

My first night alone came to symbolize the difficult journey I was about to embark on. I was forty-six years old, and everything about my newly acquired house seemed dark, cold, and empty to me. Why did I buy it? Because it was the only one in my price range I could even begin to consider. It had vague potential for becoming a cozy little solitary retreat, but when I moved in, the smell of puppy pee in the corners of the living room was undeniable.

Having recently embraced a deep and desperate need to get beyond the soul-obliterating grasp of my soon-to-be ex, being anywhere seemed better than listening to him lecture me one more time about how inadequate a human being I was. That night I lay in my suddenly too-wide queen-sized bed, shivering at the prospect of my future. I still had my job, my shelties, and a few human friends. All was not lost.

Every time I tried to nod off into the lovely, forgiving escape of unconsciousness, the roar of the furnace called me back to full attention as it switched off and then on again. It felt like the entire room vibrated when the blower came on, whooshing like a miniature hurricane beneath the floor. Would I ever adjust to everything that had changed in my life?

The next morning I started the slow process of accepting what I had gotten myself into. The forty-year-old linoleum in the kitchen was the first thing that caught my attention. There was so much grime stuffed into those cracks it made my stomach queasy. So, I thought, this is what a 75 percent reduction in take-home pay feels like!

The Dreaded Double Ds: Divorce and Depression

My first few months went by in a blur of loneliness and despair. Focused on how I might brighten up my dark little home while also shedding some light on my compromised disposition, I began to renovate those parts of the house that I simply could not stand.

As it turned out, solar tubes were just the thing, so I hired an attractive man to come install one. While we were both up on the roof, I noticed his broad range of practical skills, which went well with his nice broad shoulders. He simultaneously told me the age of my roof and assessed its condition while expertly putting in my skylight. The thought did occur, how nice it was to have a handy man around the house. I even attempted a tiny bit of flirting, but he told me he was already involved, so I quietly filed away in my rattled brain: "Next time, get a partner who knows how to fix things!"

In the spring I explored my new backyard for garden potential and found lots of it. I started visiting local garden centers and learning more about native plants and xeriscape. I would nurture a native plants garden. That was what I needed! Gradually, as my little seedlings popped up, I got happy. My memories returned of how independent I had been before my marriage. I wanted my old self back, but with interest. I remembered that I had always been a strong, resilient woman who had weathered many a tough winter and always found the wherewithal to bloom again in the spring.

Occasionally I still felt tortured by questions about my past. *Why did I stay so long in such a destructive marriage? Did I really value myself so little?* Divorce gave me lots of time to think about past choices. In the process I gained a powerful appreciation of my right to escape from a hopeless, demeaning marriage.

On the Mother's Day following my divorce, I gave my mom a call to thank her for giving me the strength of character and the integrity to move on when my marriage lost its love and became destructive.

Renovation Times Two: Home and Self

Focusing on my home always brought me back to the present and helped me keep my many internal struggles at bay. I spent about a year sitting out back on my nasty, poorly constructed screened-in porch contemplating the pros and cons of converting it into a bright, warm sunroom. Noticing the great southern and eastern solar exposure, I decided this porch definitely needed a makeover, just as I needed a new project to help me feel better about myself and my difficult circumstances.

With help from a few friends, I first removed the old, rotted walls, leveled the roof, and then respaced and reinforced the support posts. After adding all new glass and insulation, I installed inexpensive pine paneling to cover the inside ceiling and solid wall surfaces. The old cement slab floor was the next eyesore that had to go. As soon as I could afford it, I hired a friend to place some handsome, moss green tile in my new solarium. Then I started growing lots of interesting cacti and succulents out there, because they were unique and colorful and could handle the cooler winter temperatures.

The benefits of adding a glassed-in room to the back of my house were immediately obvious. On a sunny winter day, my sunroom warmed up much faster than the rest of the house, and by the afternoon I could open up my sliding door and direct the extra heat inside. It became my favorite place to hang.

And far beyond the economic and eco-friendly advantages of this small addition, my bright, festive sunroom cheered me immensely. Since I had nowhere else to put the clothes dryer, I moved it into a hidden back corner of the room.

Then, on those days when it was too cold to hang out the laundry, I added a little extra humidity by turning it on, thus creating the "Caribbean effect." With reggae music blasting and a margarita in hand, I would give myself a free virtual vacation by pretending I had just arrived on a luscious, verdant tropical island for a relaxing stay!

The metaphor was not lost on me. With the transformation of my old house and sunroom came the renewal of my own spirit. One renovation led to another. Most mornings you could find me sitting in an old rattan chair drenched in sunshine, my Shetland sheep dogs scattered at my feet, writing in my journal and plotting my next great transformation. If I could do this, I could do anything!

Unfortunately, my rising spirits hit a nasty snag two years later. By that time my divorce was safely behind me, my little house felt like a real home, and I was feeling pretty good about myself.

Throughout the emotional turmoil of divorce, my job as a reference librarian had been a reassuring, stabilizing constant in my life. Then, one day, my boss called me into his office to inform me that he didn't wish to renew my contract. I was shocked. I was forty-nine years old and had never lost a job. But now, after twenty-five years as an academic librarian, I was apparently disposable.

My initial reaction was anger and tears. How could I endure another major setback? Why did these things keep happening to me? Although things were looking pretty grim, I'll never forget the gift I received as I drove home from work that day. I was in great distress, wondering how I would ever find another job, and then from somewhere deep inside a voice calmly announced, "This change will probably save your life."

So I decided to reframe this crisis into an opportunity. For more than a decade, I had been halfheartedly trying to transition into a different career. Perhaps this was my once-in-a-lifetime opportunity to change everything at once.

Severance pay and unemployment checks provided me with a few months to myself to confront some of my deepest fears and demons. I began to question every choice I had ever made. This was my chance to expand my mind and my options. What had I missed by making the decisions I'd made? What aspects of my true self had I tried to ignore all these years? What parts were now begging for proper attention? I was on a journey to fully understand the first half of my life, to make the second half better.

Risky Business: Finding Love Later in Life

Living on the edge like I never had before, I knew my safest move was to find work in librarianship. But I wanted more. Back and forth I struggled in my mind, between doing the "safe" thing and trying something new and exciting. My intuition kept telling me to watch one of my favorite movies, *Risky Business*. I finally did, and then I knew why. The famous line, "Sometimes you just have to say 'what the fuck,' and make your move!" spoke directly to me.

I would pursue my own version of a risky business. Since I hated my options for dating and I definitely needed a job, I started my own matchmaking service for those over forty. I chose to offer a highly personal option and spent hours interviewing every client, getting to know them well enough to fully understand their needs. I loved my time with them, and the experience also brought up brand-new challenges within myself. After marriage had turned out to be such a disappointment, did I still believe in love?

Through my business, I arranged lots of fun activities and met many decent, interesting people looking for love later in life. I even had a few success stories as a professional matchmaker, but I didn't meet anyone special for myself. Still, my clients' hopes and dreams, and their willingness to put themselves out there, gave me the impetus to do the same.

I began to sit in my safe, grounded sun porch and read old cards and journals from decades past. I was on a quest to understand love, why it lasts and why it doesn't. I wondered if I had ever truly experienced romantic love in my life, and became focused on the one that got away.

No, not my ex-husband, heaven forbid, but a ruggedly handsome mountain climber I had lived with and loved in my early twenties. We were together for only a couple of years in the late 1970s, and it had ended badly, but while it lasted, it had been my first taste of unconditional love. Where was he now? Why had things gone so wrong between us? How could I still believe that love was possible after so much disillusionment and disappointment?

Against all my better judgment, I felt an overpowering urge to call him up. I could not get him out of my head. He had a distinctive name, so I had no problem finding his address and phone number, but should I? I tried writing him a simple, nonthreatening letter first, but never received a reply. I waited a whole year and then wrote again. Still, nothing.

So one bright July morning, while sitting in my sunroom for fortification, I casually gave him a call. Twenty-five years after our last conversation, he sounded fabulous! He even seemed pleased to hear from me. We had always found it easy to talk with each other, and that hadn't changed. We spoke for a couple of hours about the many years that had passed. It all felt so warm and familiar. And at the end of the conversation he said, "Thanks for calling—you made my day!"

We continued to talk over the next month or so, and I slowly fell back in love with him. At first, I held out hope that love might return between us. But as we spoke, I realized this was not the reason for our renewed bond. For decades I had blamed myself for the failure of our love affair. He now told me the truth, how severe depression had ruined his relationships and ruled his life. He apologized for the trauma he had caused in mine.

Talking to him was reassuring. I was now absolutely certain I had not squandered the best love relationship I had ever had. Bless him for having the patience and courage to share his truth with me and listen to my accumulated anguish over past rejection. Our talks unearthed many years' worth of excruciating pain, which then flowed out in one gigantic, cathartic wave of relief. I finally felt healed from decades of self-blame and ready to love again.

Since I wanted to start dating, and hadn't met anyone so far through my efforts, I decided to join Match.com. I figured I would create a general online profile, meet some nice men, and then tell them about my dating service if we didn't click. I certainly had my doubts about online dating, but I didn't know where else to turn. At first I received few responses, and it began to seem hopeless. I was ready to just give up. Then I received a wink from Mike. He was wonderfully responsive by e-mail, awfully nice on the phone, and lived only ten miles away. I invited him over for a visit.

I covertly peered from behind my curtain as he walked up to my door, trying to decide whether to hide his big flower bouquet behind his back. I was touched. With a great smile, he introduced himself. His moniker on Match.com was Tall Guy, and he was right about that—lanky and lean in a very sexy way. I fell into his eyes almost immediately and thought I would never get out. Those greenish-gray eyes! I simply couldn't resist telling him within minutes how beautiful they were.

We sat in my sunroom for hours, talking, laughing, and quickly discovering the many things we had in common. We had both lived in Asia in the 1970s and '80s, he in the Navy, I as a China specialist. The conversation felt soothing and comfortable, like talking to an old friend after many years apart.

Within about an hour I felt relaxed enough to reveal my practical side. I ventured, "You know, I'm very good with money." And he responded, "So am I!" We both knew we had met someone very special that day. He loved my sunroom and its imitation Caribbean charm, and soon afterwards realized he also loved me. I was falling in love again at forty-nine!

As our relationship developed, it became apparent that I would need to sell the little ranch house I had transformed so lovingly. This was traumatic. The house, and especially the sunroom, had come to represent my personal triumph over adversity. But my feelings were also strong for the "tall guy," so I took the plunge and staged my house for a quick sale a few months after I met Mike.

The first buyer who walked in wrote a contract on the spot for the full price. I had improved the value of my house by $20,000 in four short years, while reviving my own spirit, and all in a very eco-friendly way.

I spent many a long, lonely night in that cold little house, but I'm still so glad I left my first husband (my "wasband," I like to call him). It was time to be brave and take my life back. Divorce takes time, to regroup and decide what's next, what needs to go, and what definitely must be kept. It builds strength and character—if we can only find the personal courage to stand alone and endure whatever comes our way.

Mike and I married eight months to the day after we met, convinced that soul mates do exist. Our wedding was elegant in its simplicity—a quaint, intimate gathering of family and friends in our rose-filled backyard. When we spoke our precious words to each other, all in attendance wept.

It's Never Too Late to Find Out Who You Might Have Been!

This new and powerful source of confidence-building acceptance soon blossomed into a once-in-a-lifetime opportunity for me to consider a real career change. Mike was the first of many new friends I made during my midlife crisis who stubbornly worked to convince me that my childhood fantasy might have some real potential as a money-making venture. At last I had the right combination of time, courage, and energy to embrace my destiny. I decided to become a writer.

Looking back, I see clearly that none of the many positive transformations in my life could have happened without that first brave decision to divorce. I needed to stop settling for less than I deserved, stop playing it safe, and end the pattern of unconsciously compromising myself and my own needs. It was time for me to learn a powerful new form of compassion and respect, and start giving this to myself.

What Is Midlife?

Looking around a busy Barnes & Noble recently, I noticed they had specially delineated sections for teens. Struggling through the crowd, I finally got the attention of an attractive, dark-headed twenty-something assistant and asked, "Do you have a special section for midlife?" He turned to me and said, "What's that?"

Astounded, I didn't miss a beat. "Readers in their forties and fifties. You know, in the middle of their life."

"Oh no," he said, "those are grouped with the other adult nonfiction books." And then he smiled the cutest smile and wandered off.

I was astonished by the education I'd just received. What's midlife, you ask . . . just wait!

Midlife seems to surprise us all, much like the other transitions we may experience in life, like divorce, menopause, or unexpected layoffs. We go along, thinking we have things mostly figured out, and then, *bam,* we're struck silly by some gigantic change we didn't even see coming. Welcome to the midlife wake-up calls that inform us, in not-so-subtle ways, that it's time to figure it out all over again!

But then, that *is* pretty much the point, isn't it? We need to be shocked into the realization that we haven't figured it all out. There's so much more to learn before this game is over. And if we're slow learners, life just keeps coming at us until we finally get it. What would it take to wake *you* up?

It took a divorce, hysterectomy, and the first layoff of my entire twenty-five-year career to wake me up.

The divorce was the first blow. It left me wondering, "What was I thinking? Did I really think I could spend the rest of my life with him?" Time to reevaluate all the choices I'd made up until then. The good news is that it caused me to delve into my previous beliefs about love, call up an old boyfriend from twenty-five years past, and finally get rid of lots of accumulated guilt and shame.

My second major change was a hysterectomy. This turned out to be the best medical decision of my life. I remember my doctor asking me to describe how I felt about my uterus. I said, "It's been nothing but trouble my whole life!" She said, "Right answer!" and we proceeded to the planning stage of my surgery.

The layoff was the toughest blow for me. I had clung to my identity as a librarian for decades, not because I loved the work but because I needed that one bit of security in my otherwise precarious world. When that final bit of stability fell, I was completely on my own in the dark and lonely sea of midlife transition. Strike three, you're out!

And I was out, out in the world completely on my own with no husband, no job, and no uterus. What's a girl to do? I began to dwell on the question, "How did I arrive at this place?" Taking care to avoid the stickier question—am I really just a loser?—I decided my entire belief system needed a remake.

That was the beginning of a wild and crazy journey for me, one that has led to all sorts of changes, and all for the better.

Midlife Confusion: What's a Girl to Do?

I was deep in midlife confusion and decided I was desperate to call that old boyfriend, the one I hadn't spoken to in over twenty-five years. At the same time I was dealing with major menopausal crying jags and hot flashes, not to mention inexplicable urges to buy sexy lingerie for the first time in decades. I was certain that I had flipped my lid.

I called my older sister to check up on my scary state of mind. It was such a gigantic relief when I described my symptoms to her and she said, "Sure, I did all those crazy things too. Those are the classic symptoms of a midlife crisis. Didn't you know? There are whole channels on cable devoted to this kind of behavior!"

Great, I thought: If this is normal, the whole world is in trouble. Think of all of us baby boomers losing it at once!

The one burning question for me was this: Do I still believe in love? After all the mind-boggling disappointments life had thrown at me in the past few years, could I honestly feel positive about love coming back into my life? And if not, what was the point?

I had briefly tried a few online dating services. My advice: Carefully protect your self-esteem if you plan to venture into that avenue of modern life. And remember, everyone seems to find it way too easy to lie to themselves and others online. I suppose for most of us it's just another resource for midlife confusion. But that's a whole other story . . .

As for the old boyfriend, talks with him were quite revealing and healing for me, but he ended up being as disappointing as he always was. I eventually got my hot flashes under control. And the lingerie came in handy sooner than I expected.

Is This a Midlife Crisis, or Does My Life Just Suck for Now?

Sitting at a table full of older women at the Colorado Authors' League, I mentioned the Midlife Crisis Queen and everyone cracked up. I had definitely hit a nerve. And we all agreed that it is really not clear what midlife is. Seeing as none of us knows how long we'll live, we decided that midlife is whenever you think it is.

Speaking for myself, I was deep into my crisis before I realized it. One thing just led to another until I was up to my neck in alligators. I think the experience that defines a midlife crisis is all the internal questioning. *Why am I doing this job? How did I end up here, now? Why do I live here instead of in a place I could love? How did I ever get so stuck in this routine?*

I'm reminded of one of my favorite sayings ever:

> The only difference between a rut and a grave
> are the dimensions.

The most important question eventually arises: What would it take to wake you up?

I think midlife is an excellent time to reevaluate everything—to revisit all the choices you've made and why you made them. Are they still the best choices for you? Midlife for me was a desperate attempt to understand the beginning of my life better, so I could make the second half different.

There are excellent reasons why we made those choices back when we did, but most of them don't match where we are now, because we chose from a place of fear and insecurity. Now we've grown and it's time to take full responsibility for ourselves and our lives. No more blaming others. What do you need to happen before you die? It's a simple but oh-so-important question to ask yourself over and over again until your heartfelt answers come through.

This is the purpose of a midlife crisis, to wake you up to all the choices that are right in front of you. Are you angry or frustrated with the way things have turned out? Empower yourself and choose something different! Nobody else can do this for you.

The Dreaded Double Ds

The holiday season is the worst time for the double Ds to come up, yet they are common at this time of year. My divorce began, so to speak, on Thanksgiving in the year 2000. Why do I remember? Because it was also my husband's birthday, and we had a gigantic argument about his birthday cake, of all things. Like everything else in our marriage, it wasn't perfect enough for him. That was when we finally agreed, at exactly the same moment, that it was time to call it quits. Happy holidays!

This made for an even more joyous Christmas season, as you might guess, and New Year's was a blast! While I launched into a depression of colossal proportions, my soon-to-be ex kept up appearances with friends and acted like nothing was happening. In some ways that was the worst part. Perhaps he was simply relieved that I was finally leaving, but he could have at least acted upset about it.

Trust me, you don't want to go looking for a house to move into right around Christmas. The selection was limited, especially on my budget. Don't people know that they should at least clean up the dog poop in the yard before they show the house? But I was desperate to get away from living with a man I only wanted to escape from, so I settled too quickly on a run-down but almost adequate little house.

Then, since my soon-to-be ex was a real estate tycoon, and I had no experience buying or selling houses, he came with me to secure the loan. Imagine the scene of me crying in the loan officer's cubby while my ex managed the loan process with absolutely no sign of emotion. The female loan officer got it, even if he didn't!

One of my most depressing memories of that time is from my job: struggling not to cry at the reference desk while waiting for the next question. Hanging out at the fast-food restaurants near the library, I could no longer contain my tears. Now that was a pathetic scene—crying into my Big Mac!

My sister suggested antidepressants, and they helped a little, but the thing that helped me the most was getting totally wrapped up in planting a beginner garden from scratch in my new backyard and then remodeling my house. Becoming active in helping myself, instead of only focusing on the hopelessness of my situation, empowered me.

I want to share with you the best advice I received during that time of severe depression. Richard Gere appeared on a talk show and his wise words seemed to speak directly to me: **"Hang on, it all changes!"**

Truer words were never spoken! I couldn't have imagined how much my life would change after that very difficult time. I only know now that none of the wonderful changes I've been through in the past few years could have occurred without that painful period following my divorce.

Know When to Walk Away, Know When to Run

*If you settle for less than you deserve,
you get even less than you settled for!*

How much energy have we all put into wishing our lives were otherwise? How many times have we wished our spouses or children were just a little less like who they are? Perhaps we simply don't like our lives, our choices, our jobs, our spouses, and rather than taking full responsibility for the choices we've made in the past and the ones we'll make today, we start blaming others.

Blaming and shaming those around us because we hate our lives is no solution to our problems, but that is a great summary of my first marriage. I married the king of blame and sometimes called my marriage Criticism Central. Things were not perfect at our house, and according to him, it was typically all my fault. Let me tell you, that's a recipe for disaster!

I think I learned the most about self-responsibility while watching that well-educated, intelligent man blame all his problems on everyone else. Do you realize how unattractive an adult can be when he takes no responsibility for any of his choices?

What I'm describing is classic emotional abuse. If you happen to be in the middle of it, get out before your self-esteem is nonexistent! If you need more information to decide whether you're being abused, read *I Closed My Eyes: Revelations of a Battered Woman* by Michele Weldon.

Up until the time I read this book, I blamed myself for staying too long in an emotionally abusive marriage. I felt I had no excuse for my behavior. I was well educated. I had a career. I had options. Why did I remain in such a demeaning situation?

Michele also had options, but it took her a long time to realize how insidious domestic abuse can be. It wears down your self-esteem bit by bit until you feel complete despair and hopelessness and crave the slightest signs of acceptance or love.

After my separation and divorce, I decided it was truly time for me to grow up. The day came when I could no longer blame anybody else for anything in my life. That kind of confrontation with reality is both terrifying and revitalizing. I now call it "taming my victim dragon." I decided to take charge of my life. If I fail, then I fail. But if I'm happy or I end up successful, I have only myself to blame!

Feeling like a beginner at age fifty ain't easy, but believe me, I'm just that stubborn. The whole time, the phrase *with no visible means of support* kept flashing through my mind, like in that old Playtex commercial.

The Process of Escaping Emotional Abuse

Once you start changing things in your life, how do you know if you're headed in the right direction?

How do you even begin to change when you know your life isn't working? My advice, if you feel hopeless, alone, and like a gigantic failure: start anywhere you can.

I parlayed my post-divorce depression into a warm, vibrant sunroom, but first I read Michele Weldon's life-changing book. At one point in her saga, Michele broke through her despair long enough to paint the walls of her dining room the mellow shades of cantaloupe. The change cheered her up immensely.

This gave me an idea. What if I transformed that nasty, run-down screened-in porch into a bright, sunny space just for my own pleasure? I didn't have much money, but I had lots of dedication to the project. That porch represented my weakened spirit. It needed a remodel.

At this point, Michele's words spoke to me like none ever before:

> Deep down in the transmission of my soul, I needed to make a change you could see, something that would last for years, if necessary, and be a reminder of who I really was: a woman who was not always and permanently afraid, a woman who could change. I needed to see for myself something positive that I had done, a move that was not born out of hurt but strength and creativity.

I remember sitting at lunch with a friend and crying as I told her just how revealing this book was to me. It was like holding a mirror up to my soul, and not liking what I saw.

Perhaps if I could transform my physical environment first, that process would give me faith that I could also change my internal beliefs about myself and where I belong in this world. It was worth a try! I knew I needed to change, and I saw no other way out.

So I dug in, and out of sheer stubbornness and determination I made it happen. I created a warm, safe place for me to sit and plan my ultimate escape from my self-destructive outlook.

The new addition to my house gave me a strong, solid foundation where I could begin to build a better future for my damaged soul. All the essential changes that came into my life after that—finding a new love, discovering right livelihood, and my powerful, loving sense of self-respect—germinated and grew to maturity in that sunny, nurturing greenhouse environment.

> Rock bottom became the solid foundation I built my future success upon.
>
> —J. K. Rowling,
> author of the *Harry Potter* series

I Said I'm Divorced, Not Contagious

A major contradiction in our culture is the illusion that there's no longer a stigma attached to getting divorced. Oh, come on! It's a nice party line, but it's absolutely false.

When I got my divorce—which was a completely friendly transaction with no lawyers; all healthy, adult agreements—I lost a number of my so-called friends and I definitely felt judged by others. All of our couple-friends went to my ex, and one new-found "friend" ended up unable to continue seeing me. She was probably afraid that divorce is contagious, like the measles.

At dinner parties, I was that eccentric single person. And it became increasingly clear to me that mentioning experiences that involved my ex was not appreciated. Unfortunately, that included most of the experiences of the past ten years of my life. I had no problem with my divorce, but obviously others did.

In her truly great book, *Around the House and In the Garden: A Memoir of Heartbreak, Healing, and Home Improvement,* Dominique Browning concludes:

> Divorce is its own sort of disease . . . and it carries its own threat of contagion. People shun the divorced woman: she might make you too sad; she might sicken your marriage; she might give your husband ideas. I will never know if these attitudes are figments of my imagination, or real—I can only compare notes with others in my position, and see that we're not too far apart in our perceptions.

Perhaps it's mainly women who get stigmatized by divorce. "What's the matter—couldn't keep your man?" The assumption being that any man is better than no man at all. Come on—we can do better than this, people! Few marriages are matches made in heaven, and sometimes they truly need to end.

Mismatched is no match at all. It's only fair that after a mistake, each of us can try again to find happiness before it's too late.

Divorce: A New Cure for TMJ

Back in 2000, all in the same week, a huge wildfire started just over the mountain from the house my husband and I had just purchased, I had a major breast cancer scare, and the back window of my car was shot out while I was driving.

How's that for stress? My life, my home, and my car were seriously threatened all at the same time. I'll never forget going out on the porch and seeing a gigantic, billowing smoke cloud rising over the hill behind us.

That same week, my dentist suggested that I needed help with my unconscious teeth grinding, which was causing TMJ. I followed his advice and spent $300 on a special appliance to wear at night. I ended up not wearing it much because it was so uncomfortable.

Just recently, I woke up thinking about that time in my life. I realized suddenly that I no longer have any stress in my jaw. In fact, I feel more relaxed and happy than I can ever remember feeling.

This brought up a funny thought. I saved it up to tell my dentist. The next time I was in his chair, I said, as best as I could with his hands in my mouth, "Do you remember recommending that mouth apparatus for my TMJ?" He said he did. I said, "Next time, you should first ask if your patient would consider a divorce, because my divorce was the perfect solution to my teeth-grinding problem!"

The Loss of the Dream

Sad to say, I find myself to be a bit of an expert on divorce. It certainly wasn't my intention to know so much about it, but there it is. The first thing I learned from my own experience and from talking with hundreds of others is that divorce is *always traumatic.*

When my husband of six years and I decided to call it quits, we went about it in a very civilized and "adult" way. We both agreed that we were making each other miserable, we had tried various counselors, and we were simply too different in our goals and interests to stay together. In other words, it was a purely rational decision.

Unfortunately, my emotions didn't agree. I was crushed and felt emotionally disabled. I felt like the biggest failure in the history of womankind. Meanwhile, my soon-to-be ex seemed to cruise through this difficult time with ease, and his apparent inability to feel anything just made things worse for me.

I quickly launched into a midlife crisis of astronomical proportions, asking myself all the tough questions. *Why can't I "do" marriage? What is it about me that makes me unable to be with others emotionally? Do I have to live alone forever? Why doesn't love last?*

As luck would have it, just two years after the separation and divorce I lost my job, intensifying the depth and drama of my ongoing crisis. Then I had to ask myself even more difficult and searching questions: *What am I doing here? Will I ever find meaning in my life? How do I want the rest of my life to be different?*

I got so wrapped up in this quest, I decided to start my matchmaking service to explore the simple question, "Do I still believe in love?" while helping other recent divorcées with their own explorations. It turned out to be wonderful therapy for understanding my own feelings about love and rejection.

First of all, I learned that I most certainly was not alone in my disillusionment with love. There are millions of baby boomers out there who don't know how they feel about love and relationships. Interviewing scores of disillusioned divorcées showed me that we all have a lot to learn.

It became clear to me that we learn more about a person by divorcing him than we could ever have learned by staying married to him. When we're married, we're always "playing nice" to some extent. We still have a lot invested in the relationship and its future. When divorce becomes real—and it takes each of us a different amount of time to register this disturbing reality—the gloves come off and we become more honest with our soon-to-be exes. There's no more relationship to protect, so, naturally, we begin protecting ourselves and our own interests. In short, we say what we've been thinking all along.

A singles workshop I offered to my dating clients provided a moment of awakening for me. We were discussing the contradiction between the simple, clear rationality of divorcing someone we no longer love and, on the other hand, the deep emotional emptiness that can take hold after the reality of it all sinks in.

A short, elderly gentleman, who looked a bit like Sigmund Freud and spoke with a heavy German accent, stood up and said, *"Divorce is not about the loss of a relationship, it's about the loss of the dream."*

Truer words were never spoken. I had not only lost a significant human connection in my life, but, more importantly, I had lost faith in love and the beauty it can bring to an otherwise difficult existence. For what is life if we fear that we will never feel true love again?

I knew then that I had to get busy and turn my heart around. I needed to find a way to believe in love again. In my case, this wasn't an easy assignment. But I took all the necessary steps and love did return, more of it than I could ever have imagined!

The Causes of Midlife Change

One of my blog readers asked me, "Can a job loss cause a midlife crisis?" My answer is that *anything* can cause a midlife crisis.

Whatever causes you to begin to question *everything*, every small choice you ever made that led you to this moment of unhappiness—that's a midlife crisis.

Don't get hung up on semantics: "Am I in midlife? Is this really a crisis?" Just accept the gift in front of you. This is your chance to change something important, and your body and soul are begging you not to miss out on this golden opportunity.

By the time a crisis happens in your life, as defined by your own gut feeling and intuition, it has been cooking inside you for quite a while. For example, my ex and I were working up to a divorce for years before we finally did the dirty deed. It takes lots of courage to finally give up and admit failure.

And I can now see perfectly in retrospect that I unconsciously willed myself to lose my job, too. It and most of the people I worked with were toxic; it was a negative environment for me. Every time I commuted to Denver, I attempted once more to convince myself that it was a good job I really should feel thankful for. But somewhere deep inside, "the still small voice" was shouting at me, "This is a nine-to-five way of dying!"

My unconscious finally took care of it for me. And believe me, learning I was losing my job made me very upset. But I'll never forget the voice I heard on my way home after being told I no longer had a job. A voice came through loud and clear as I headed north out of Denver that day. It said, "This will probably save your life."

Listen to that still small voice, no matter how irrational it may seem at the moment. It is a gift that will protect you in those difficult transitional periods like divorce or unemployment.

One important lesson I learned is that life goes on . . . even for the unemployed. I guess I thought life just couldn't go on as usual, but it did. I still got up in the morning, ate my breakfast, walked my dogs, and spent time considering my options, but I found my options had expanded greatly. I had somehow gotten out of the mindset of doing the same old job for the rest of my life, and now I could do anything! So what's next?

This is where solitude was essential for me. Spending lots of time alone forced me to look inside and begin to study my life and my choices. What were my natural skills and talents and how could I use these to be a force for good in the world? Nobody else could tell me the answer to this question. This was my own personal conundrum.

The time alone taught me many things, but especially self-responsibility. There was no one around to blame for this crisis in my life. Life was simply being what it is, and I was at an important crossroad.

Eventually I would realize that this precious gift of time alone with me was the completion of a learning cycle. It was my golden opportunity to change in midstream.

Solitude

*"And you, when will you begin that
long journey into yourself?"* —*Rumi*

Loneliness scares most of us quite a bit; in fact, it may be our greatest fear. But I believe there's a lot of power in knowing that you can live alone successfully.

Living alone for a few years, especially during or after a major life transition, allows us the time to process change. We finally have some time to breathe and search within for what's missing or what definitely needs to change. As luck would have it, midlife often offers this time to rest up from relating to others constantly. Divorce, a loved one's death, unemployment, an empty nest, or some combination of these common midlife circumstances can offer a natural breather to sit back and take a hard look at ourselves and where we are.

If you're anything like me, you've been constantly distracted by the needs of others. As natural caretakers, we just can't stop tending to the needs of those around us, even when we aren't being asked for help. That is why it's so important now to find a way to spend some time completely alone.

Your tendency may be to immediately find new distractions, new people to care for. Fight that impulse. After a lifetime of chaos and caring for others constantly, this is a very important time for you to be alone, as scary as it may feel at times. How else will you have the time and fortitude to face yourself squarely and ask some tough questions about your previous choices and your future?

Introspection demands solitude and time. This may be why many of us never truly get to know ourselves until midlife, if ever. It takes a lifetime to know ourselves well. The only way to your true self is through contemplation. No shortcuts are available on this one. You may find that a good therapist is a great guide at this time, but the heavy lifting must be done by you. This is the beginning of self-responsibility. Up to now, life has just happened, and in the chaos of it all you've done the best you could. Now, if you choose, you can take full responsibility for your life, for your own process, for all future choices, and for your own solitude.

Why is solitude so important? We cannot learn and grow without personally processing what we alone have experienced within the context of our own lives. No one else understands our own internal experiences of loss and alienation quite like we do, and no one else processes these experiences into wisdom like we can.

Without personal processing at a deep level, we will continue to make the same mistakes over and over again. We all go through periods of crisis—major changes, intense difficulties—as we age. It's best if we can intersperse these episodes with periods of solitude and deep learning, to integrate and consolidate what we have experienced in preparation for a new learning cycle.

If we learn with each cycle, we become wiser and more able to cope with the next difficulty. If we never stop and spend some time alone, integrating lessons learned, we cannot accumulate wisdom or the ability to live a more comfortable life with more supple and adaptive coping skills.

Self-Discovery 101

After my divorce, I began to focus on getting back to my own needs and goals in life. The best name for that daily pursuit is self-discovery. Every day I would read this question on my fridge and give it some thought:

If you could have, do, or be anything right now, what would you ask for?

Keeping this question in front of me helped me realize the boundless possibilities I had to choose from. It also reminded me to choose wisely this time. I could see that I was in the midst of a classic midlife crisis, especially after I lost my job and was living on severance. Through my matchmaking service I met a man who gave me a better term for my experience: middle-escence. Much like adolescence, middle-escence is a time of confusion when we are filled with questions like, "What do I want to do with the rest of my life?" and answers are in short supply.

Life becomes more precious as we age, and we don't want to waste any more time settling for less than we are, or deserve. But how much do we dare dream? Can we really live our dreams, or is the desire to do so pathologically optimistic?

This is my list of things I want to accomplish before I die:

I would like to become my best self, letting go of more of my fear, anxiety, and illusion of control.

I would like to discover, honor, and contribute my best skills and talents.

I would like to find more fun and meaning in my life.

I hope to find right livelihood for myself.

The world needs assistance in improving human ways of relating. I believe this is where my contribution lies.

I think Jesus said it best in the Gnostic Gospel of Thomas:

If you bring forth what is within you, what you bring forth will save you. If you do not bring forth what is within you, what you do not bring forth will destroy you.

Getting to Know the New You

One of the best possible outcomes from a midlife crisis, and perhaps the true purpose of these major transitions—whether divorce, menopause, job loss, whatever—is the adventure of getting to know the New You. Try to enjoy the adventure of getting to know your new self as it emerges.

So much has changed since you first married or chose your career. Spend some time remembering where you were psychologically when you first met your spouse or decided to become whatever you are now. If you're lucky, you might have a journal to remind you what issues were important to you then. Most likely, security was way up on your needs list back then, and fear a major motivator.

Contrast that with what is important to you now. What do you love now? What are you passionate about? What do you *have to do*? Do your best to visualize a new life that includes these loves, realizing that the picture will most likely come to you in small pieces, like a puzzle. Keep the faith that each piece will arrive just in time to take you a little closer to the future you envision for yourself.

Then start noticing the tiny signs in your life that subtly lead you toward your dreams. These are signs that you might have previously called coincidences. Pay attention to them; see where they lead you. For example, once I decided I really wanted to be a writer, a writing conference turned up in my town just in time, and I learned about it through pure serendipity, from a bulletin board at our senior center.

Notice the signs in your life and the patterns coming at you. The clearer your vision of a different future is in your head (or on paper), the more signs will emerge. Use all the tools and resources available to you to learn more about the change you think you might like. Try the Internet, blogs, self-help books, local groups and programs, music, exercise, every avenue you can think of to encourage your creativity and growth. Whatever works, use it!

Now is the time to find new courage within yourself for change. The more hopeless you feel, the more strength you must find inside. Keep your eyes on the prize! And remember the wise words of Wayne Gretzky: **"You miss 100 percent of all the shots you never take."**

Life Transition: Crisis or Opportunity?

We've all experienced it. Either by choice or by chance, the time arrives when we know we need to gather together enough courage to make a major life change. Whether we've recently joined the ranks of the divorced or empty nesters, or have experienced a change in health status or a layoff at work, a life transition is upon us. How will you weather this new storm and come out the other end in better shape than when you started?

Don't despair! Though it may feel like the end of your world, there are many resources available to ease your fears and help you find a much better fit for your future.

If these changes begin in our forties or fifties, we may suspect that it's time to rethink our previous choices but wonder if we have the courage to follow through on something so risky so late in life. Most of us don't consciously choose to put ourselves through this kind of stress and anxiety, but change happens.

My time of crisis began in my mid-forties. With a divorce at forty-six and job loss at forty-nine, I thought my life was over. Instead, it was just beginning. These unforeseen misfortunes created an opening for me to change everything and thus transition into a more positive life purpose. With my training in counseling psychology, I knew enough to know what I could change successfully on my own and what I would need extra assistance with.

First, I started my matchmaking service. Although this enterprise was not ultimately successful, I learned a lot about my skills and interests. Then, at age fifty, I decided it was time to move on to a new career. This is where outside assistance was essential for me. Throughout my twenty-five years as a librarian I always assumed that I would change careers when I discovered the kind of work I really loved. During those years, then, I pursued the proper training to transition into a career in counseling psychology and also subconsciously nurtured the dream of becoming a professional writer.

But I needed an outside expert to soothe my deepest, most irrational fears and convince me that professional writing truly was a "real job" that was perfect for me. It took my career counselor months to convince me to give writing a try. And when I finally did, I loved it! I even found I had some natural abilities and talent for the work. The counselor just had to convince me to briefly suspend my disbelief around what was possible. This freed me to pursue the dream I had always nurtured but had been too frightened to follow through on.

This made me start thinking about the larger-than-life fears we all confront daily, fears that can keep us from getting what we want and need in life. Even though mine was a career change, similar fears can stand in the way of our pursuing any transformation that could potentially improve our fundamental quality of life.

A Life-Changing List

Here are ways for you to feel the fear but still pursue your best dreams and intentions for your future:

Trust in your inner wisdom and your power to change.
Acknowledge that all change is a slow process that can make you feel uncomfortable at times. Try taking baby steps toward change, while also embracing the risk taker inside.

Give yourself permission to experiment and explore. It's normal to run into dead ends. Just don't let them stop you.

Don't be afraid to ask for help through a difficult transition. Consider hiring a coach or a counselor to push you through your own personal stuck spots, to help you admit what you truly want and go after it.

Use all the tools and resources available to you: self-help books, local groups and programs, music, exercise, creativity, whatever keeps you on your path of self-discovery.

You're not in this alone! Network! Enlist the help of friends, family, and colleagues.

Don't give in to your biggest fear of all, that you are a loser or a failure.

Realize that the picture of your new life will most likely come to you in small pieces, like a puzzle. Maintain faith that each piece will take you a little closer to the future you envision for yourself.

Enjoy the adventure of getting to know your new self. So much has changed within you since you first married, had children, or chose your present career. What do you love now? What are you truly passionate about?

Make use of solitude and journaling to nurture yourself, question your old beliefs, and figure out where you need to go next.

Suspend your belief system just long enough to get exactly what you want this time—no more worn-out old rules. Hang on . . . it all changes!

What to Do If You Feel Like a Midlife Loser

I'm beginning to think that feeling like a loser is one of the primary symptoms of a midlife crisis, as well it should be. How many people make sweeping changes in their lives if they feel like things are going as planned?

But is this a crisis or an opportunity? Don't despair! Be glad that it's finally time to do things differently. We despair when we believe that we can't change, but that is wrong, wrong, wrong! I am living proof that you can turn your life around whenever you become miserable enough to shout, **Enough of this nonsense! I want a different life right now!**

The more you want it, the more likely it is to happen.

The first step is to recognize exactly what is *not* working. You've trusted in the sensible, practical side of your brain all these years, and look where it's gotten you. Exactly where you don't want to be! Now it's time to take a leap of faith and start to pursue your heart's desire, which includes everything you thought you couldn't possibly have.

In other words, it's time to start taking risks. Analyze it to death if you must, but eventually the day will come when you need to take a gigantic, scary leap of faith and begin reaching out for the life you've always wanted. How can you know your dreams are impossible if you don't at least give them a shot?

I'm not talking about a half-assed attempt here. I don't mean "kind of" pursuing your dreams. I mean reaching out for *everything*, on the off chance that it's out there for you. This means reaching inside yourself for as much courage as you've ever had. Fight like your life depends on it, because it does! Stand up for yourself and take a stand for your own integrity and self-respect.

Decide what you must have before you die in order to feel good about your life. Is it one marvelous relationship? Is it a creative impulse you've tried to ignore all these years? Is it lots of money? Is it world peace?

Whatever it is, don't talk yourself out of it this time. Be completely honest with yourself. Enough of those irritating little voices in your head telling you that you don't deserve what you really want. You get to win this time—it's now or never!

There's no one else to blame for where you are right now, and no one to save you from the fate of mediocrity, except yourself. Are you up to this challenge?

Getting Beyond Mediocrity

Ever since I read his book *Still Me*, I've been inspired by the heroism and intelligence of Christopher Reeve. I'd always loved his acting and his choice of roles. I also envied his clarity of purpose: "While I was growing up," he recalls, "I never once asked myself, 'Who am I?' or 'What am I doing?' Right from the beginning, the theater was like home to me. It seemed to be what I did best. I never doubted that I belonged in it."

Being someone who has doubted my purpose just about every day of my life, changing college majors and even master's programs numerous times, I've always been impressed with those who know exactly where they belong in the scheme of things and hold close to that vision.

Christopher gained a whole new perspective from his experience with crippling disabilities, and he observes later in his book, "Most able-bodied people are too complacent, too easily satisfied with mediocrity."

I completely agree, especially after living with a man with chronic fatigue syndrome—an unpredictable and punishing disability. Most of us take our own health for granted, don't even exercise regularly, and complain about everything that doesn't come easily.

Somehow we all got the impression that life should be a breeze—so how come mine isn't? One of the gifts of my midlife crisis was the discovery that I would have to fight for a better life for myself. I did pretty well at mediocrity through my forties, but I wasn't happy. I learned that to excel, I would have to really want something and work harder for it.

The struggle began with simply figuring out what I really and truly wanted. What *would* finally make me happy? That was enough of a challenge, because I have a hard time allowing myself to dream. A powerful quote from Christopher Reeve spurred me on:

> So many of our dreams at first seem impossible, then they seem improbable, and then when we summon the will, they soon become inevitable.

As optimistic as this may sound, I have found this to be very true. First we must embrace our dreams and make them ours, turning off all those bothersome doubts that would have us never try anything new and different. Don't you think I was scared to death to change careers or even to start dating again? You bet! But then I heard those spunky, crazy, wise words from the teenager in the film *Risky Business*: **"Sometimes you've just got to say 'what the fuck,' and make your move!"**

Shame on You for Changing Your Life

The worst part of any major transition is the shame con-
nected to it.

Most of us like to think that a mutually agreed-upon divorce or simple job layoff is not shameful. But something in
our culture and deep within our own psyches begs to differ.

My own divorce felt quite shameful. I can see now that
any divorce, no matter how mutually desirable, creates trauma and feels like a failure on some level. Of course, it doesn't
help that the people around you may start treating you differently. Some of my women friends actually dumped me after
the divorce. Obviously their greatest fear was that one day in
the not-so-distant future they might end up just like me.

I really fought the feeling that I was a failure, and it sure
didn't help that the bottom fell out of my standard of living.
How depressing to have to move into an old, cold, dumpy
little house because my ex had made most of the money in
the marriage while I was keeping the home fires burning. At
least I still had a good part-time job. It was my saving grace.

While fixing up my house slowly, as I could afford it, I
nursed my sad and shame-filled soul until I started to feel
a bit better about myself. Then, out of the blue, my boss
laid me off. Another blow! I grieved for a while and then
reframed my situation in my own mind. I changed my crisis
into an opportunity. Screw them all, I was going to survive

and thrive through this transition! The kind of stubbornness
created from pure anger really helps in situations like these.

How to Fight Midlife Disillusionment and Depression

The first step in this journey depends entirely on how depressed you are. If you think you may be suffering from a
serious depression, please read the definition of clinical depression in the next chapter; if you have those symptoms,
reach out for professional help immediately. However depressed you are, seek help. Don't take no for an answer. Keep
at it until you find someone you like, someone who can truly
help you feel better about yourself and your life.

Sometimes we just need to know there's help out there,
people who care and will do whatever they can to keep us
safe until we can make changes in our lives and begin to feel
better on our own. Don't let your fierce sense of independence fool you. *We all need help sometimes.* Take care of your
deep need for understanding and support *right now.*

Once you feel rational and relatively stable, begin to gather
around yourself the friends, pets, books, music, movies, and
other things that help you feel better about yourself. Begin
to create your own space where you can enjoy sitting alone

contemplating your life. Silence is important, but music can also help at times. You don't need a lot of space, just the kind that feels peaceful and nurturing to you.

It is now time to find out who you are. Beyond all the messages you've been receiving your whole life, beyond the influence of every person you've ever spoken to or anyone who has shamed you, there's a unique soul inside that needs to be heard right now. Your job is to excavate this person for the first time and recognize him or her as your best self.

What do you love? What activities free your soul? Do you love color or sunshine, exercise or music? Do you get really excited about the first blossoms in spring? Who are you now?

There is no past, no future, there is only this moment.

With solitude and a complete openness to learning, you may begin to gain essential self-knowledge, knowledge of things that only you can know about yourself. A counselor or therapist may be helpful, but in the end you are the expert on you. So dig deep and find out who you are and what you need to do now.

Midlife depression is often caused by a depressed ability to access and express your true self. Enough of living your life for everyone else! Your friends and family may be important in your life, but sometimes you must also acknowledge your own unique needs and talents. This is an opportunity for your true self to emerge. Listen to its wisdom. This may be your last chance to get what *you* need out of your life.

Once you have a clearer picture of how you want your new life to proceed, create a plan either in your mind or on paper. Decide what your priorities are. Is a job change your highest priority? Or changes in your closest relationships? Perhaps your highest priority is simply to start exercising or begin painting or journaling again.

Pay attention to all the little clues around you. What books or music do you keep hearing about? Check them out! As new people come into your life, learn what you can from their wisdom. Talk to those you trust about your new perceptions and explain why you need to change now. Perhaps they can assist you on your journey.

Plug into the world around you and trust that you are on your very own path to self-knowledge and self-empowerment. Change can feel so good sometimes!

Defining Depression

A recent multinational study found that, regardless of nationality, gender, marital or parenting status, or income level, people are more likely to experience depression in their forties than at any other time in their lives.

What is clinical depression, anyway? According to the fourth edition of the *Diagnostic and Statistical Manual of Mental Disorders,* the bible of psychological diagnosis in many countries, **a major depressive episode consists of five or more of the following symptoms during a single two-week period:**

Depressed mood most of the day, nearly every day

Markedly diminished interest or pleasure in all, or almost all, activities most of the day, nearly every day

Significant weight loss when not dieting, or weight gain, or decrease or increase in appetite nearly every day

Insomnia nearly every day

Psychomotor agitation or retardation nearly every day

Fatigue or loss of energy nearly every day

Feelings of worthlessness or excessive or inapproriate guilt (which may be delusional) nearly every day

Diminished ability to think or concentrate, or indecisiveness nearly every day

Recurrent thoughts of death with recurrent suicidal ideation without a specific plan, or a suicide attempt or a specific plan for committing suicide

These symptoms must cause clinically significant distress or impairment in social, occupational, or other important areas of functioning, and not be the direct physiological effects of a substance, such as drugs or a medical condition.

I give you this information because I know many of you are in your thirties, forties, and fifties, and may be experiencing depression right now.

Please seek help! You don't have to go through this alone.

There are people with extensive training who can work with you to improve your life. This is not the end of the world, simply the end of this part of your life. Your body and mind are telling you that things need to change for the better, and your first step toward that change is to seek help from those who really understand what is happening inside you. They can give you the help you need to move on to a much better stage of life.

Why are we more vulnerable to depression at midlife? There are many good reasons—physical, spiritual, and emotional. We have generally done what we were told up until now. We got a job or career, got married, perhaps had kids, tried to live the American dream.

At midlife we begin to see that one size definitely does not fit all. Our unique and amazing true self emerges and starts to make all sorts of demands. Our intuition, the voice within, or our gut feeling tells us that we have lost our way. Up until now we may have ignored the voice within, but now it starts speaking loud and clear and it won't take no for an answer.

It tells us to follow our bliss, find our right livelihood, seek out the love that we've been craving our whole lives. We deserve this, for once! It takes a lot of energy to ignore this voice. Best just to give it a listen and see where it can take you.

Dealing with Anger

Most of us in midlife have questions about dealing with anger, and I think I know why. Perhaps you were raised in a house where the expression of anger was basically not allowed. Maybe only your dad was allowed to get angry, and the rest of you scurried around trying to avoid becoming the target of his rage.

If that's the case, you may have a deep, even preverbal fear of expressing your anger. It took me a couple of years of counseling to realize I had no access to my anger. Whenever I started to get upset, I became uncomfortable. I would suppress it as best I could, but sometimes, if it kept coming, I would have trouble breathing.

I ended up going to an anger workshop, whose purpose was to teach us how normal it is to feel angry. Anger can be the best indicator that the self is being abused, and we are correct not to take that lightly. Our anger may show us where our lives are not working and wake us up to where they need to change. The leaders of this workshop also pointed out that without anger there can be no joy. We are meant to have the full range of emotions.

Sometime after that workshop I had one of those revealing moments that you never forget. I was driving on the highway feeling terrible about the way my husband treated me. I was listening to a tape about anger and suddenly I started crying so uncontrollably that I had to pull over. There on the side of the road I slowly realized that underneath my sadness and pain was a gigantic reservoir of anger and frustration.

Women tend to hide their anger—even from themselves—within their pain and depression, because sadness is more acceptable in women than rage or bitterness. Men often have the opposite problem, because demonstrations of anger are more acceptable for men than crying or depression.

I felt ashamed to be angry. It was somehow unacceptable. I think I actually feared this response, because during childhood it could lead to bodily harm. But I came to this awareness as an adult, and as an adult I could allow myself my full range of emotions, which freed me up to simply feel my anger. The anger indicated to me that I needed to change my life circumstances in some major way.

It's very important to monitor your bodily responses to the things in your life. Your body knows long before your mind registers when you're being treated unfairly, when you're feeling stressed, when you need to defend yourself. Learn to listen to your body—and listen carefully!

Having access to all your emotions is a big part of living an authentic life. Be aware of how you might be censoring various parts of yourself. Training in self-censorship starts very early, so it takes time to welcome back those parts lost in your upbringing.

Anger with Yourself

The most difficult time for me after the divorce was the time I spent kicking myself for staying too long in an abusive situation. I was upset with myself because, when I got completely away from my ex, I saw so clearly how I had wasted years of my life on him. What a ridiculous martyr to the cause!

This is where I began my struggle back to some sense of love and compassion for myself. I realized that we're all only human and have only our limited backgrounds to fall back on. We were born completely innocent into this world and our parents raised us the best they could. In some cases they taught us to play the victim. That's simply the way it is. That was all they knew.

Now we have this amazing opportunity to do things differently and the awareness to make our lives better this time. Lucky us!

Self-compassion is an important life skill you've always needed and need even more right now. Blaming and shaming yourself is as useless as blaming others. Be here now, and then move on to the best life you've ever had. Explore and learn more about your unique and precious self now. What do you love? What gives your life meaning? When you take full self-responsibility you then take charge of creating your best life ever.

After much contemplation I decided I wanted more fun in my life. I hadn't had much fun for a few years and I wanted to make that happen. So I focused completely on what I alone thought was fun. I came up with being in the sun, walking my dogs along the river, meeting other older singles, writing in my journal, anything to do with color and creativity, following my intuition blindly, loving myself instead of always criticizing myself, and fixing up my house.

Give yourself what you've always needed and no one else has given you: true human acceptance. Start out repeating this affirmation to yourself: **"I love you and accept you exactly as you are."** Then move on to this one: **"Wow, you are fabulous!"**

Nobody else can fix this for you. You and you alone can do this for yourself. This is true empowerment.

Why this Identity Crisis Now?

What brings on the increase of depression in our forties?

I got a great clue from reading the book *The Gift of Fear* by Gavin de Becker. This book explains how humans are the only animals that will consciously decide not to listen to their instinct or gut feelings when they are in the presence of danger. His best example involves waiting for an elevator. It arrives, but it contains a person who immediately gives us the creeps. Human beings are the only animal that will ignore strong warning signs from within and go ahead and get into a soundproof steel box with a scary person.

I've observed this with my dogs. If they get a bad feeling while we're walking, they simply stop and go no farther. They did this once on the edge of town and I soon realized a coyote was watching us from a distance.

The question is, how do we get so out of touch with our self-preserving instincts whose purpose is to help keep us out of harm's way? I think the answer is the same as why we wait until midlife to revisit our innate inner wisdom and sense of self.

It seems to me that most of us spend the first half of our lives learning how *not* to listen to our instincts and intuition, and the second half relearning the wisdom of this inner voice.

"Do What You're Told!"

Being raised in a culture means being taught to follow its rules. Life would be chaotic without most of those rules. So, as children, we need to learn how things work and why we should do as we're told. Often the rules can protect us from harm. But somehow, eventually, these same rules take on a life of their own. The rules become an excuse for not thinking for ourselves. All the pressures of life may converge upon us to marry at a certain age, have children, take the secure and sensible job, and try to leave our gut feelings behind.

Challenging the Rules

At midlife, our original instincts may reemerge and inspire us to say, "Wow, what was I thinking?" A powerful desire to retake control over our lives and destinies may emerge from shocking occurrences like the death of a loved one, divorce, job loss, or change in health status.

We may decide to quit playing it safe and start living the rest of our lives exactly as we see fit. This I call the dawn of self-ownership and self-responsibility.

Depression and Change

Not surprisingly, in the midst of this transformation, we may feel a lot of anger and frustration with having "wasted" so many years coming to this realization. This may culminate in a time of depression, as we navigate a passage out of the old patterns of denying our inner wisdom and into a renewed sense of self and purpose. We may need to revisit previous relationships, change the conditions of present relationships, change jobs, move, or even change our entire image to accommodate this change that comes from within.

This is *not* a cheap excuse for treating others badly; in fact, it's the opposite. It's a time to step up and begin treating ourselves and everyone else in our lives with the dignity and respect we all deserve.

Life and Suffering

For to resist life's ubiquitous and inevitable
impermanence is to suffer, and to accept change
with compassion is to transcend suffering.

In the depths of my midlife slump, this self-created saying reassured me immensely. I needed to remind myself daily that change was inevitable. This too shall pass. "Hang on, it all changes!" were the words I needed to hear to believe in a better future for myself.

At the worst of times, it is damn near impossible to believe that things can change at any moment, but they can. This is an important lesson from Buddhism: Everything about life is impermanent. And to try to make any of it permanent is an illusion that only leads to suffering.

This is a very tough life lesson, but worth acknowledging every day. The bad news is that all you are attached to today will pass away, including yourself. The good news is that, as difficult as your life may seem at times, it *will* change.

We live in a society that denies suffering while pretending that all is happiness and light. Pain is not our forte as Americans; denial is. Many industries have been built up around denying unhappiness and suffering. Even the funeral industry is in denial of why it exists. Few films allow bad things to happen to people and then deal with the aftermath of suffering.

Books and music are some of the best places we can turn to when things get tough. Good books don't deny that people suffer and die and can offer some great solace in dealing with all the emotions involved in grief.

Societal denial makes acceptance of suffering even more difficult. Others may not understand how to be with you in your most difficult times because we all pretend that bad things don't happen. Only a few of my best friends were able to be with me through my toughest times. They could handle being around my immense sadness with compassion and acceptance. More typical was the close friend who made it obvious she couldn't be with my pain; she changed the subject and then went to get her clothes out of the dryer.

Accepting change with compassion begins at home. Give yourself heartfelt love and compassion when you screw up, when the marriage doesn't work out, when you lose your job, when you know you've done your very best but things have fallen apart anyway. Remind yourself that you're only human.

Self-compassion takes time and practice. But if you can find a way to recognize that you are fundamentally good and worthy of love, then the next step is to love yourself fiercely.

Try to love yourself for all your successes *and* your failures, through thick and thin!

Selflessness vs. Self-Respect

No matter how hard one searched, one
could not find anyone in the universe more
deserving of love than oneself. —Buddha

Most of us were raised with an understanding of selfless behavior, especially if we were raised female in this society. What is selflessness? It is the belief that it is normal and healthy to take care of the needs of others to the extent of ignoring our own selves and our needs. It means we never develop a strong sense of who we are, separate from those around us. We never feel that we have the right to appreciate our unique qualities, what we love about ourselves, and what we hate about our lives.

Examples? They're everywhere! Many of our mothers and fathers took care of us selflessly. They sacrificed, they scrimped and saved for us. This is where we learned the behavior. There are wonderful examples of self-sacrifice in our culture. Look at many of the heroes in the newspaper and on TV.

What is self-respect? Knowing and loving ourselves well enough not to let other people dump on us or manipulate us. Unfortunately, many of us were manipulated so much growing up that we consider it normal. We feel guilty simply for treating ourselves with love and respect. If somebody around us needs something, we're there to help, even if we're ill, have no strength left, or have bad feelings deep down inside about those we serve.

Just think about the term *self-sacrificing behavior*. Does that sound like a healthy choice to you? It can only lead to more guilt, manipulation, and martyrdom. It doesn't feel good inside.

People with healthy self-respect care very deeply about the needs of others. But they also know where to draw the line when others demand too much. They know that it's not satisfactory or advisable to go through life without a healthy sense of self and boundaries. In fact, doing so can lead to serious depression and even total self-destruction through illness or mental breakdown.

The key is to learn to give from a place of having enough, rather than from a place of guilt, shame, or desperate need for love and attention. Learn to give because you love yourself and feel abundance in your life. Give because it gives you joy, and not because you'll punish yourself later if you don't.

Confusion about this leads to lots of frustration, sadness, and anger.

"How do I distinguish my reasons for helping in the moment? Helping others just comes naturally for me. I love helping others . . ." Only *you* will be able to distinguish your true feelings about your natural "need" to help others. If you find yourself saying, "I do so much for them and they just don't appreciate me!" you may be erring on the side of selflessness.

It sometimes helps to think in terms of your own needs versus those of the other. If you can begin to think of yourself as a separate person, someone outside yourself who desperately needs help, you may then begin to feel compassion for yourself and your own needs. You may begin to believe, *"I have as much right to love and compassion as anyone else, don't I? What do I need right now?"*

The sure sign of selflessness (also sometimes called codependency) is doing for others what you most desperately wish someone would do for you. If you feel alone, lost, and in need of compassion, you try to give that to someone else in hopes that the favor will be returned.

Why not try asking directly for what you need next time. I've found that by asking those I love for what I need, I almost always receive it—and at the moment I need it, too. If they can't give it to you, reconsider who your loved ones are. If they don't treat you with love and respect, perhaps they have no self-respect themselves, and don't deserve your endless outpouring of love and care.

Are You Trying To Save Others, When You Really Need To Save Yourself?

One of my dysfunctional tendencies is the desire to try to help those who don't really want my help. This seems to come from a deeply felt need to feel useful at all times, plus a natural ability to see flaws in others much more clearly than those in myself.

Even in some of my most desperate moments, when my personal survival has been at stake, I've reached out to others to try to "help" them. As they successfully thwarted my efforts, I still stubbornly demanded to be there for them. Now of course, the assumption that I would know better than they did what needed to happen in their lives, especially at times when my own life was falling apart, is silly. But sometimes it's felt like I could only redeem my own life by saving theirs.

It's not as if I didn't know that no one can ever really save another's life. We all must find the strength within to go on living. We must decide for ourselves what life is worth to us. These can be transformative moments, when our lives do truly change. We may realize on a much deeper level that we want to stay here and try to make a difference.

As I look back over my life, I recognize that on a number of occasions my stubborn need to "fix" someone else has actually been my own well-disguised cry for help. These attempts were so well disguised that I couldn't even see them myself.

It was only when the person I wanted so desperately to help rejected all my efforts that I was confronted with my own depression, loneliness, and anguish. I was forced to look at myself in a new way, and things didn't look good!

This realization has presented a new kind of freedom to me. I will never again try to help or "fix" anyone who obviously doesn't want my assistance. I will love myself instead, and put my energy into those endeavors that improve my quality of life on many different levels. I will assist only those who love and support me and my efforts in the world, and try to keep myself and those around me as happy and healthy as possible.

Crisis and Personal Change

Why does it seem that most of us need to have a breakdown before we experience a breakthrough? For me, it's only when I've pushed myself too far in a direction my Self doesn't want me to go that my whole body, mind, psyche revolt and say to me, "OK, that's enough of this!"

For example, when I was in my twenties, I thought I was invincible in the independence department. I moved all over the country alone, changed colleges four times so I could study what I wanted, and changed boyfriends regularly so I didn't get too dependent on any one relationship. Self-sufficiency was a major theme in my life.

In 1982, I moved to Ithaca, New York, on a year-long scholarship in Chinese language study, and then followed it up in Taipei with a scholarship at the Stanford Center. That's when my luck ran out.

Living in Asia was an alienating experience for me, especially with few close friends around. The Chinese liked to stare and point at us funny-looking foreigners while commenting to their friends in Chinese (which I could generally understand) on how strange we all were. In addition, a few important people died or abandoned me during this period of my life.

It was a very tough year for me, and I finally had to admit to myself that I was starting to lose it. It was the year my independent spirit took a body blow. I returned to the States with my tail between my legs, feeling right on the edge of a mental breakdown.

Finding our own personal edge is important in life. Pushing ourselves to the edge of our tolerance helps us understand more clearly what we're made of. Sometimes we learn we're much stronger than we ever imagined, but we may also learn that we need to pay closer attention to our emotional needs and respect our intuition.

I learned that I really did need the love and support of those around me. More importantly, I learned that I needed to begin to give myself proper love and respect.

At the suggestion of a friend, I started seeing a counselor soon after returning to the States, and this long-term relationship changed everything. My therapist challenged my rugged individualism and my seemingly contradictory codependency. I would sometimes fight others off while at the same time trying to manipulate them into being my friend. Talk about mixed messages! I was getting nothing of what I wanted and needed out of life. I felt cheated and alone.

It seems that I needed to push myself beyond my limits and bring myself to a crisis before I could see the contradictions in my behavior. Only when I had arrived at a crisis did I seek help from someone who could see and understand my whole complicated dynamic and how it had developed.

Even now, twenty years later, I still think those therapy fees were the best-spent dollars of my entire life. My life simply wasn't working and I was miserable. Breakdown eventually led to a much-needed breakthrough in self-awareness and self-esteem.

Honor and Celebrate Your Own Power to Change

I can't do it, I can't do it. I don't know how to do it.
I wish I could do it.
What should I do? I think I might try it. I might do it.
I think I can do it.
I can do it. I will do it. I am doing it!
I did it!!!

Breaking the barriers in your own mind, convincing yourself that you can and will do what seems absolutely impossible today—that defines your power to change your life.

It starts from self-ownership and huge self-respect. It starts from accepting yourself exactly as you are. A few years ago I began to wonder if I really accepted myself so fully. I realized that I'm not what society would like me to be but that I am absolutely unique in this world, for better and for worse. So I made a list of all my qualities, a long list. It included qualities like strong, independent, stubborn, courageous, emotional, creative, diverse in my interests, empathic, passionate, nontraditional, analytical, rebellious, critical, painfully honest, direct, trusting, loyal, and funny.

The deeper question was, "Who am I apart from the things that define me?" I'm not just someone's daughter, sister, or wife. Away from my family, job, and friends, who am

I? I spent some time alone with this question, undistracted by life in general, and answered it for myself.

I also made a list of everything I'd like to do before I die and prioritized my answers. I was shocked to find that list a few years later and realize that I had accomplished most of the goals on it.

I started to really enjoy hanging out with the new me, the brave person who is exactly who she is regardless of societal input. Of course, I also lost my job when I let my true self show, but it was a toxic work situation that needed to go.

The World's Fastest Indian, with Anthony Hopkins, is a fabulous movie about an old coot with the apparently impossible dream of breaking the land speed record on his 1920 Indian motorcycle. A true story, the guy actually made it from New Zealand to the Nevada salt flats and finally reached his goal. One line from the movie stays with me:

> You've got to take a risk now and then to make
> life worthwhile.

Why not begin today nurturing your true self and your dreams? Step into your own worth as a person. Make a list of everything you would really, deeply like to do before you die. Don't limit yourself or your goals. You are the world's best authority on you. Decide who you are and live that life now. Time's a-wastin'—all you have to lose are your regrets!

Self-Acceptance and Appreciation

How many of us feel perpetually inadequate and insecure? How many of us crave genuine acceptance, or even simply being seen by those around us?

How did our world ever come to be this way? Must it always be like this?

I think not. If we could stop for just a few minutes each day and focus on loving ourselves and appreciating all that we already have in our lives, the insecurity might slowly evaporate.

We might lose our powerful need to have others acknowledge and reassure us of the beauty of our own existence. We might no longer feel so competitive, always trying to prove ourselves and yet needing more and more assurance from outside because at the end of the day we still feel so empty inside.

Genuine appreciation starts with the self. Appreciation for our healthy bodies, our miraculous brains, and our effortless ability to see, hear, and fully experience this amazing world we were simply born into.

If each of us learned to respond to each day with the thought that this was the first day *and* the last day of our life, how would we treat each other differently? How would we spend this day if we knew for certain that this was the last one we would ever experience?

Try to embrace the thought that everyone you meet today will be blessed by you, just by your eyes, by your smile, by your touch, just by your presence. Let the gratefulness overflow into blessings all around you.

Self-Acceptance: We're All on Schedule

I once took a workshop with a famous self-help leader at the Naropa Institute. I can't remember her name, but I'll never forget this one thing she told us: **We're all on schedule!**

As much as we wish we were further along in our lives, in our careers, within ourselves, this is where we are now. The first step to moving beyond this moment is fully accepting ourselves right here and now.

This is particularly relevant to career change. When I began writing professionally, I hated feeling like such a beginner. But that was exactly what I was. It boggled my mind to think of all the amazing writers who had been working on their craft for years, even for decades, while I was just starting. In fact, for years I had regularly talked myself out of trying to write. I'd read a phenomenal book and then say to myself, "See, I could never do anything like that!"

And you know what? I was right. I couldn't have written those books. They weren't what I needed to write. They may have been wonderfully illuminating for me to read, but they weren't my own personal passion. It's been a slow process for me to try various types of writing, to be told that personal essays don't sell and then continue along that avenue anyway.

As an engaging young English professor told my writing group recently:

> When you find your passion, you'll know it, and
> then nothing will stop you from pursuing it.

Too bad we get in our own way so much of the time. We don't stop to listen to the wisdom from within. Somewhere inside, despite all the outside noise, we know what we need to be doing with our lives. It takes a large dose of self-respect, courage, and self-awareness to follow this one true path.

We tend to get in our own way because, in part, we're angry at ourselves for falling behind those around us. We compare ourselves to those we wish to be more like. Always a mistake! We need to respect our unique qualities and begin to listen to our own wisdom, not someone else's. We're exactly on schedule for the lessons we're learning now, lessons that will propel us to the next level of wisdom and understanding.

One of the bonuses of midlife transitions is that we may begin to see how this cycle works in our own lives and then finally give ourselves credit for being exactly where we need to be right now.

If we don't accept and embrace ourselves in this moment, why should we in the next?

It's like a dog chasing his own tail. It may be entertaining, but it doesn't get him anywhere.

So try setting your intentions for complete self-acceptance today. See how that changes your perspective. You are exactly who you need to be today. Embrace that thought!

Each day we are born again. What we do today is what matters most.

Don't Let Past Relationships Ruin Future Ones

I kept a fairly detailed journal of my personal journey after my divorce. Reading through it recently, I was surprised that even a couple of years past the separation, I still felt depressed and damaged by staying so long in an abusive marriage. Fully two years after the divorce I wrote, *"The two beliefs I gained from spending too much time with him are: All men are jerks, and no one would ever want to be with me because I'm too much trouble . . . I'm flawed."*

When I read this later, I was furious that I had let him have so much power over me and how I felt about myself.

Going through a major breakup is devastating, even if you have no love left for your ex. I spent a few years kicking myself for staying with such a jerk. Only then did I realize that he was moving on, and that it was high time for me to do the same. I needed to find a way to let go of all the false assumptions I had adopted by spending so much time with him.

Finding self-love is the only solution to feeling flawed and unlovable. For me this required spending quite a bit of time alone, getting reacquainted with myself. Not with the self that had stayed in a bad marriage too long, but the self that loved to walk her dogs along the river and do watercolors and remodel her house into a place she could love. The self that was strong and resilient and ready to find love and happiness again. I had to love myself into believing in future love.

Then I had to convince myself that not all men are jerks. My dating service worked well for this. Through my service I met and interviewed many men, a few of whom I really liked. I remember one day when I interviewed three different men. On my way home from the last interview, my intuition came through loud and clear. It said, "My heart is back alive. I like men again!"

Good friends convinced me to give love another try, and I'm so glad I did. Feeling loved and appreciated is an incredible gift worth working toward.

Finding Your Passion

We've all seen those silly articles about "reinventing yourself" and "reigniting your passion for life," but how do we really change things? Where to begin?

I'm reminded of a statement I heard years ago: *When you don't know what to do, do nothing.* If you feel truly stuck and without any real direction in your life, it's time to take a cold, hard look (and feel) about where you are right now.

To me, this is the gift of midlife. We have enough experience and self-knowledge to know what works and what doesn't work for us. Now we just have to have the confidence and honesty to decide what needs to happen next.

Try becoming wildly courageous on your own behalf. Jump outside your well-defended security perimeter and do something you think you can't do. You may learn how boundless your powers really are!

You probably can't imagine how scary it was for me to start my own business after working as an employee for twenty-five years. I felt extremely exposed. But I went with my gut and took what felt like a gigantic risk. And though my business wasn't particularly successful and I ended it after six months, I learned a huge amount about myself, what I love to do, what I don't love, and I built up confidence for my next attempt at getting what I want out of life.

No one else knows exactly what you should be doing right now. But I would venture a guess that, somewhere deep inside, *you* know—if you could just learn how to listen.

Gather enough courage to listen to that part of yourself today, even if it seems to make no sense at all. Even if it isn't really what you should be doing, it may still be the beginning of your path to self-ownership and self-responsibility.

Listen to the voice within and give it a chance to communicate. Give it the time and space to whisper in your ear, perhaps through journaling, conversations with friends, or a career coach or counselor. Pursue this personal secret as if your life depended on it, because it may!

Celebrate Self-Responsibility

Misunderstandings about responsibility create much unhappiness in the world. Most of us have learned negative connotations to the idea of "being responsible" or "taking responsibility."

Taking 100 percent responsibility for ourselves is one of the most important steps toward genuine self-respect and love. When we take less than 100 percent self-responsibility, we operate from the victim role ("Take care of me, I'm inadequate"). When we take more than 100 percent responsibility, we're operating from the rescuer role.

Responsibility is best taken as a celebration, not as a burden. It is a freeing act to take responsibility for ourselves. When we do, we take back power over our own happiness.

You can only take action in this moment. Childhood is over. Instead of focusing on what somebody did to you in the past, focus on what you would like to create right now.

Are you playing the victim or the rescuer in your life?

Work on setting clear boundaries of exactly what 100 percent responsibility means in your present life. Don't give away your power (that is, don't play the victim), but don't try to control others, either. Just take charge of your own self and what you create in the world.

Don't blame yourself or others. Fix the problem, not the blame.

Here are some helpful affirmations for taking healthy self-responsibility:

I am completely responsible for all my own feelings and actions.

I am completely responsible for my own health and welfare.

I give others complete responsibility for their feelings and actions.

I take complete responsibility for making and keeping agreements.

I take responsibility for expressing my true essence in the world in positive and loving ways.

Is It OK to Ask for Help Sometimes?

Too many of us were raised to believe there is some kind of shame in admitting weakness and vulnerability. There are times when we really can't do it all ourselves, and we must learn to ask for help. I think it's high time we all begin to feel better about reaching out when our lives overwhelm us. This stubborn independence thing is a weight too much to bear!

We've all had those memorable moments in our lives when we knew we simply could not go on a step further. Unfortunately, in movies and books the fiercely independent heroines always do go on, like Scarlett O'Hara after Tara burns to the ground.

Movies are one thing; real life is another. Let the people you love know when you are struggling. If you need help, ask for it!

One of the most important lessons I learned from my experience seeing a counselor is that it truly is OK to ask for help. In fact, it's a far better choice than feeling unhappy, unloved, and angry that others don't just intuitively know when you need a boost. It's an important part of self-nurturing behavior. So take full self-responsibility!

Perhaps this can be your new midlife resolution:

I will ask for help when I need it, instead of feeling like all my problems are always only my problems.

Coping with Uncertainty

To err is human; to forgive, canine.

So why does our generation have a high and apparently increasing suicide rate? Why does it seem like everyone I meet takes antidepressants? Are we the damaged generation?

Actually, I believe it's the opposite. I believe we're one of the most aware and well-educated generations of Americans ever. And with awareness comes responsibility.

We understand that depression and chronic fatigue are not character flaws but the consequences of genetic and environmental factors. Who wouldn't be damaged by combat in the Vietnam War? Who wouldn't get depressed if their body stopped working for no apparent reason and with no way to fix it?

We're a generation that feels responsible for everything, even what we have no control over, and that's a recipe for crazy. It took me a couple of years of counseling to see the overwhelming degree of responsibility I felt for a world I had little control over. The same is true when raising kids. We feel totally responsible for their health and welfare, yet how much of their world do we really control?

I had to learn to let go of my illusion of control a number of years ago. I had started having mild panic attacks in public. I wondered what everyone around me was thinking.

I wondered how I would make it through each day. I learned to comfort myself by going to the worst-case scenario. I'd ask myself, "What's the worst thing that could happen in this situation?"—and then realize that I could survive even that scenario.

Very reassuring . . . but today, the worst-case scenario has definitely gotten much worse. Especially when our government plays upon our fears constantly. If we watch the news and know how much craziness is out there, we may wonder how our world goes on as normally as it does. How do we get up each day, go to work, have a home life in the midst of all these wild events?

I like what author Jodi Picoult has to say on this subject. She's had lots of life challenges. Her kids have serious health problems. She says, "How do I cope? The way each of us copes with uncertainty: By celebrating what I've got, instead of waiting for something else to go wrong."

Each of us has to make a number of decisions every day about our attitudes. I've learned to err on the side of an affirmative view of humankind. I try not to be too hard on myself or others, to keep busy doing what's important to me, to stay focused on the positive, and to somehow embrace the many uncertainties around me. Sure, anything may happen, even something surprisingly good!

Take the Risk of Being Positive

When things are looking pretty grim in your life, it can feel scary to try to imagine something better for yourself. Part of the reason for this is that you may have an unconscious belief system that says, "I deserve all the bad things that are happening to me right now, and this is punishment for something I did in my past."

This reflects confusion in your belief system and a case of low self-esteem. Bad things happen to everybody. And sometimes bad things can turn into the best things that ever happened to you!

I have been constantly reminded, since my major midlife changes began, of the old Chinese fable, "The Lost Horse." In this story, a man loses his best stallion and his neighbors console him by saying, "That's bad." Eventually the horse returns with a mare by its side. The man's friends gather around and say, "That's good!"

A couple of years later, the man's son breaks his hip while riding the stallion. Everyone assumes this is very bad luck, until a foreign army comes to conscript every able-bodied man for service and his son is saved by his injury.

This allegory is the perfect description of how hard it is to interpret immediately the meaning of major changes that come our way.

One important lesson I've learned from my midlife transition is that it's impossible to interpret the meaning of each life experience as it happens. I can look back on many experiences that seemed so discouraging when they happened. And then, a few days, weeks, or months later, I realize they were just what I needed at the time.

For example, after I started my matchmaking service, I realized that I just wasn't attracting enough cool men in their fifties and sixties to match with the many dynamite women I had met. I didn't know if I could continue without convincing more men to join.

I decided to write a really general profile on Match.com to attract lots of cool older men for me to meet. I figured I would meet with them, see if we clicked, then if we didn't I'd tell them about my dating service and the many fascinating women clients I could introduce them to.

The first man I met this way turned out to be my new husband! Those initial fears about maintaining my business led to much happiness for both Mike and me.

From these kinds of experiences, I've learned that it's always best to risk being positive, no matter how discouraging your present circumstances may appear. Bad experiences often lead to something better just around the corner. The "meaning" of what is happening right now may not be revealed for a long time after it happens.

Life is shaped by all the choices we make each day. So why not err on the side of interpreting things in a positive light? Your negativity may be standing in the way of your seeing all the amazingly wonderful things that *could* happen to you today!

Midlife and Gratitude

Have a sense of gratitude to everything,
even difficult emotions, because of their
potential to wake you up. —Pema

Boy, is it hard to feel grateful when it seems like your whole world is falling apart!

Even though I knew without a doubt that I had to leave my husband, it was still depressing. It's one thing to think about giving up on a marriage, and something else entirely to pack up your life and go start over somewhere else. It just has to be tough.

We human beings seem to be built to endure great hardships. We stick with the familiar even when we become extremely uncomfortable. The miserable known somehow seems preferable to the great unknown. We tend to play it safe to the detriment of our own hearts and souls. I had to learn the hard way that remaining in my "safe" situation was draining me of all my unique power and spirit.

And even the divorce wasn't enough to teach me to respect myself and my own potential, though it was a start. I had to lose my job before I began to respect my own unique needs and ways of contributing to the world. I had to lose it all before I could find myself.

Having no job to go back to and no real opportunities to continue my career, woke me up. It helped that my colleagues who were still in the profession encouraged me not to return if I could avoid it. They were plenty sick of their jobs, too, but felt they had no options.

At the nothing-left-to-lose stage, I was forced to become more creative. I pondered and pondered the question: *"Who am I and what do I have to do before I die?"* Still, it took a career counselor a few months to talk me into being what I'd always dreamed of.

Why is it so difficult to give ourselves what we want more than anything? Because we've been convinced that we can't possibly have it all. Having it all—however we define that—may require lots of determination and hard work, but compared to what? Compared to experiencing a mediocre life and then dying?

So I now feel completely thankful for the combined circumstances that led to the loss of my first husband and then my job. At the time, it seemed like the end of my world, but now I see it was exactly what I needed to wake me up.

"You're Too Intense!"

One of the traits that brought me together with my new husband so efficiently was our equal levels of intensity.

We had both been told all our lives that we were "too intense." Have you ever gotten that line? Especially in romantic relationships, or ones that you hoped might become romantic? "I really like you, but you're too intense."

OK, so some of us aren't into small talk. That's what I loved about meeting Mike. We didn't spend much time talking about nothing. We moved right into what was important in our lives. We both also make a point of looking people directly in the eyes when we speak to them. Lots of people get uncomfortable with that sort of undivided attention.

I'm beginning to conclude that a person's level of intensity may well have to do with intelligence, because those of us who are always thinking get easily bored with people, places, and things that don't challenge us.

When I first met Mike, I found it exciting to be challenged to look at everything in many different ways. I also enjoyed how our minds seemed to move together in the same direction as we thought through an idea, and often came to the same conclusion at the same time. If you've ever found this type of synchronicity with another human mind, you know how special it is.

So don't lower your standards in your search for challenging and exciting companionship. Be yourself and be open to all the intense and unusual people out there who might just click with you.

Life's too short for nonsense. Go for intense! How can you find out whether you're compatible if you don't take a chance and launch into those topics that really matter, saying exactly how you feel about them? If you spend any time with this person, he or she will find out sooner or later anyway.

How Is Midlife Love Different?

I believe that our attitudes and romantic needs change in midlife and that the purpose of love changes throughout life.

Historically, the sole purpose of romantic love has been the continuation of our species. Without the attachment of romantic love, we would live in an entirely different society that would more closely resemble the social organization of the animal world.

The chemicals that race through our brains when we're in love serve several purposes, but the primary one is to make us form families and have children.

Once we have children, the chemicals change to encourage us to stay together to raise and protect the children. Cultural differences control how love is defined and displayed worldwide, but the fact that love exists in every human culture in the world is indisputable.

There are a few key factors that make us fall in love with a particular person. Research into attraction factors suggests that there is a template for the ideal partner buried deep within our subconscious.

Appearance: Research shows that we tend to be most attracted to those who remind us of our parents and even of ourselves. When shown digitized, morphed photos of their own faces, subjects always preferred the morphed versions of their own faces over others!

Personality: Similarly, studies show that we tend to prefer those who remind us of our parents in terms of personality, sense of humor, likes and dislikes, and various other attitudes.

Pheromones: The purpose of pheromones in the animal kingdom is to help us identify potential mates with an immune system different enough to ensure healthy offspring. Apparently, chemicals in human sweat also play an important role in love. When given males' sweaty T-shirts and asked to identify the one they felt most attracted to, the majority of females chose the shirts of males whose immune systems were the most different from their own.

Midlife Love

Obviously, when we're young and fertile, biological and cultural factors play the largest roles in determining whom we meet, to whom we are attracted, and with whom we decide to create families. How does that change with aging?

As we age, the power of biological and cultural factors recedes, and our conscious brains kick in to govern our reptilian brains.

In other words, we know whom we are initially attracted to, but then we begin asking more in-depth questions, like, "Does this person show self-respect and respect for others? Is this person good with money? Is he dependable? Is she loyal? Does he have a good record of keeping commitments?" The more our trust has been betrayed by previous relationships, the more we insist on finding satisfying answers to these questions.

We also may gain knowledge and experience in the ways of love. Perhaps from previous relationships and through the maturation process we learn that the quality of a relationship is determined simply by the way we treat each other every day.

Young love is often selfish and self-absorbed, but in mature love we are as concerned for the well-being of our beloved as for ourselves. We strive to get ego out of the way, so that we are not so critical, blaming, controlling, or hurtful. Instead, we go out of our way to ensure that our words and actions are not harmful, even inadvertently.

Truly loving another means never harboring negative thoughts about our beloved. Even if these thoughts are never uttered out loud, they become a part of the energy within the relationship.

Over a lifetime, we hope to accumulate a healthy sense of self-love and respect, which can act as our guiding light as we attempt to find positive companionship in our later years.

And that's what's different about midlife. We no longer seek the ideal partner to create children with. We instead seek loving, positive, compatible companionship.

Midlife and Imagination

In the depths of my midlife slump, this quote from Albert Einstein always cheered me up:

> Imagination is a preview of life's coming attractions.

Thanks, Albert, for reminding me that I have only to delve into my own best visualizations to see a different and better future for myself.

So let's try a little visualization. No matter what your circumstances, find a quiet place to sit alone and daydream about where you wish you were right now. Give yourself permission to cut loose and dream your best dream. Embellish as best you can! Are you alone or with someone? Whom are you with? What does he look like? Smell like? What are you wearing? What is she wearing? Come on, use your imagination!

What would be your right livelihood if you had every choice in the world? Doing nothing is not a long-term option, so what kind of vocation would free your soul? Whom would you like to reach with your unique voice and purpose? What would be your version of changing the world?

If you can't imagine it, you most certainly won't achieve it. There are no guarantees in this quest, but most of us need to free ourselves up just a bit and allow a wild and crazy dream every once in a while. What can it hurt? I found I needed this escape whenever my day-to-day reality sucked. Sometimes just putting on my favorite mood-altering music set me free.

Too bad so many of us fear daydreaming. Daydreams are just our imaginations gone wild. When was the last time you really used your imagination for anything? Why not take a trip there today and see what it has to offer you? You have to go crazy sometimes, or you might go crazy!

What Does a Self-Nurturing Life Look and Feel Like?

Sadly, too many of us have never learned how to love and nurture ourselves. So here are some suggestions for nurturing yourself in your everyday life:

Speak in "I" statements, taking 100 percent responsibility for your own feelings and actions. I no longer use the expression "I can't . . . ," but rather, "I choose not to . . ."

Take full responsibility for your own physical, psychic, and spiritual health, asking for guidance and support from others when needed.

Trust your own natural intelligence, intuition, and self-authority in making decisions that will impact your life and the lives of others.

Strive to create your own version of a spiritual practice in your life, which will center and nurture you on a daily basis.

Strive to create positive, nurturing relationships in your life that provide mutual love and respect, without either member taking more than their share of responsibility for the other's happiness. The ideal is unconditional love.

Strive to create work in your life that nurtures your own special abilities and talents while providing the world with a needed service.

Learn how to give from a place of abundance, generosity, and compassion, rather than from feelings of insecurity and scarcity.

Give yourself permission to enjoy, without judgment, any activity that you find nurturing and rejuvenating. Try out dancing, hiking, meditating, drawing, painting, journaling, music, hot springs, hot showers, writing, playing . . . whatever feels positive and nurturing!

Give yourself permission to express your full range of emotions, especially those you were not allowed as a child, acknowledging that without anger there is no joy.

Strive to ask for help when you need it. Never assume you're not worth it.

Say to yourself: I am worthy of all the love and caring that I receive on a daily basis.

Love thyself.

The Three Keys to Happiness

"I observe myself, and I come to know others."
—*Lao-tzu*

Now that I've got you daydreaming about the life you'd like to create for yourself, let's get more specific about your goals.

What qualities are key to finding some level of happiness? According to "the experts"—and there are far too many experts on this topic, considering how few truly happy people there are—three parts of your life need to work for happiness to occur.

Key #1 is the quality of your relationships.
The first relationship to consider in this regard is the one with yourself. How do you really feel about yourself? Would you want to get involved with you? What could you do to improve the way you feel about you? Answering this can take time and lots of difficult honesty. I must recommend my favorite title on this subject, *How to Be an Adult in Relationships: The Five Keys to Mindful Loving* by David Richo.

It's true that in relationships you get what you are, so try hard to cozy up to yourself and see how that feels. Look at all your relationships with this in mind. Would you want you for a parent? Would you want you for a boss? Are you taking your emotional problems out on your kids or employees?

It would do us all a lot of good if our politicians and world leaders took a good, hard look at this question.

Key #2 is the quality of your contributions.
This gets back to the old question, Are you contributing to the solutions or the problems of the world? When all is said and done, what will you contribute today? Do you feel good about what you've contributed so far? How could your contributions change and improve in the future?

This gets into the sticky problem of legacy. When people reach a certain age, they start to consider how their lives will impact future generations. Me, I live too much in the here and now to have such grand considerations. I need to feel good day to day about what I do, so I let the future take care of itself.

But one thing to think about is how often we unconsciously help ourselves when we offer assistance to others. The gratitude expressed by those we assist rewards us with a wonderful self-esteem boost.

Key #3 is the amount of control you have over your life.
I'm not advocating being a control freak, but our happiness does improve with the amount of control we have over our own time and responsibilities. Do you have much control over your own mind? Or do you feel controlled by powers outside yourself? Perhaps by fear, anxiety, or depression? Do you feel responsible for a whole lot of things you have no control over? This is a recipe for disaster.

Meditation and stress management are two of many available methods for calming our minds and taking back some control. For most of us the first step is a simple yet powerful decision to take back control over our lives by taking full self-responsibility.

Living in Abundance

Abundance is a natural state of being. It is what nature has to offer us when left to her own natural rhythms.

Abundance is how we live in each moment—with the choice to be open, the choice to entertain the possibility that we can have, create, and attract what we truly want.

Abundance is the choice to embrace each moment as an opportunity for growth and learning, within which to view the larger context—even if in this moment pain, fear, confusion, and doubt prevail.

Abundance is about faith. In time all our visions manifest. It takes faith to hold a vision.

Abundance is a choice—a choice to love ourselves and listen to the voice of our hearts. In any moment, in any situation, we can choose to exercise and express the voice of the heart or to hold it back.

Abundance is full of tests—situations that challenge our decision to live abundantly. These situations pose fear, doubt, and apparent limits. They allow learning, deeper integration, and transformation, and enable us to align ourselves ever further with our own visions of abundance.

Our bodies help us know what is right for us and what is not right. Doing something not in alignment with the heart dissipates energy. This creates a feeling of lethargy, depression, doubt, and lifelessness. This is a time to stop, meditate, reflect, and wait. It is a time to move inside rather than into action. If the body's energy becomes dissipated easily, there may be an inner lesson to learn, an inner transformation underway. This is a time to take time and space and sit with the self.

When abundance is allowed to prevail, things happen easily, naturally, in their own time, in their own way. Life is light, graceful, fun, and focused, rather than depleting.

Abundance is the lesson nature has to teach us.

Abundance can be had simply by consciously receiving what has already been given.

Midlife Redemption

"Success is the ability to go from one failure
to another with no loss of enthusiasm."
—*Winston Churchill*

What's standing in the way of realizing your dreams? Of course, you have to have a dream before you can begin to pursue it.

Some need to have a life-changing experience to find their source of redemption. For example, for decades Elton John lived the rich and wild life of a pop music superstar, strung out on various drugs. Then one day he met Ryan White, a hemophiliac kid with AIDS. This turned into Elton's life-changing moment. From this meeting he found the humility inside himself to listen to others about where his lifestyle choices were leading. He began to pay it forward instead of destroying himself.

Elton John turned sixty last year and has been clean and sober for over eighteen years. He works to spread the word that AIDS is again on the rise, especially among young gay men. And he's raised over $150 million to assist in the distribution of antiretroviral drugs throughout the world.

"Yeah," you say, "but he's rich and famous. What can I do? How can I make a difference?"

First you must find your very own passion, your unique reason to go on, and then start to assemble the support network and methods that will assist you in reaching your goal.

My moment of inspiration came in the midst of my midlife crisis. I felt like I was at the end of my rope, with very few options. I was in the depths of despair. I decided I should at least tell those who loved me what I was going through. I was pleasantly surprised when my friends and family came through for me in a big way, with lots of emotional and financial support.

A few months later I met Mike. After a horrible, lonely, and scary few years, I discovered a new love so powerful that I knew I could go on. It was a just-in-time moment for me. That's why I love the phrase, *Hang on, it all changes.* We truly never know what tomorrow will bring!

Because of my up-close-and-personal experiences with midlife crisis, I now want to reach those alone and in despair in the middle of their own crises. I want to give them the inspiration and hope to go on and find their own reason to be.

There are so many marvelous reasons to go on, to get past this low point and discover your source of redemption. I know it feels very risky. It feels risky simply to feel hope again when it may just get crushed. But this is what we humans do. We press on to greater failures until we find the unique reason we are here. And then we begin to contribute as best we can.

Good luck on your journey. May you find all that your heart desires, and then recognize it as your own!

Recommended Reading for Those in Midlife

American Psychiatric Association. 2000. *Diagnostic and statistical manual of mental disorders*. 4th ed. Washington, DC: American Psychiatric Association.

Browning, Dominique. 2002. *Around the house and in the garden: A memoir of heartbreak, healing, and home improvement*. New York: Scribner.

de Becker, Gavin. 1999. *The gift of fear: Survival signals that protect us from violence*. New York: Dell.

Gerzon, Mark. 1996. *Listening to midlife: Turning your crisis into a quest*. Boston: Shambhala.

Gilbert, Elizabeth. 2007. *Eat, pray, love: One woman's search for everything across Italy, India and Indonesia*. New York: Penguin.

Henes, Donna. 2005. *The queen of myself: Stepping into sovereignty in midlife*. New York: Monarch Press.

Josselson, Ruthellen. 1996. *Revising herself: The story of women's identity from college to midlife*. New York: Oxford University Press.

Levine, Stephen. 1989. *A gradual awakening*. New York: Doubleday.

——. 1987. *Healing into life and death*. New York: Doubleday.

Levine, Suzanne Braun. 2005. *Inventing the rest of our lives*. New York: Viking Press.

Marston, Stephanie. 2001. *If not now, when? Reclaiming ourselves at midlife*. New York: Warner Books.

Reeve, Christopher. 1999. *Still me*. New York: Ballantine Books.

Richo, David. 2002. *How to be an adult in relationships: The five keys to mindful loving*. Boston: Shambhala.

Shapiro, Patricia Gottlieb. 2001. *Heart to heart: Deepening women's friendships at midlife*. New York: Berkley Books.

Sheehy, Gail. 2006. *Passages: Predictable crises of adult life*. New York: Ballantine Books.

Shellenbarger, Sue. 2005. *The Breaking Point: How today's women are navigating midlife crisis*. New York: Henry Holt and Co.

Steinem, Gloria. 1992. *Revolution from within: A book of self-esteem*. Boston: Little, Brown.

Weldon, Michele. 1999. *I closed my eyes: Revelations of a battered woman*. Center City, MN: Hazelden.

———. 2001. *Writing to save your life: How to honor your story through journaling*. Center City, MN: Hazelden.

Printed in the United States
131502LV00002B/1/P